REBIRTHS

A VOLUME OF PERSONAL HAIKU

MICHAEL J. LEE

SHAPE DESTINY

First Edition 2021

ISBN 978-1-991200-48-8 (eBook)

ISBN 978-1-991200-47-1 (Print)

www.michaeljlee.com

www.beyondheads.com

Cover and interior crafted with love by the team at:
www.myebook.online

Contents

Poet's Preface

The discipline of the haiku format, with its three short lines, forces a poet to distil his, or her, impressions and expressions into their essence. Whether describing Nature, from its microworlds, invisible to the naked eye, to the grandeur of outer space, or capturing thoughts and perceptions as they emerge, each haiku remains beholden to the unbending rules of its creation.

In this final of three volumes, I openly celebrate my love for creation and the Creator, while encapsulating dozens of experiences and insights occurring during the period of conception. Sadly, my beloved mother passed away in this very time, following a lengthy and debilitating illness, and I've recorded a few haiku in her honour, including 113, 114, 145, 295 and 296.

Just prior to my mother's passing, I underwent a time of needing healing, from burn-out more than from anything else, and I found my peace again in the bushveld at Addo Game Park near Port Elizabeth. I've included a few poems about the wonder of witnessing many creatures living at one with their habitats. The African bush can de-stress a person like few other environments I've known in my life and travels.

But the experience of time, so crucial to the haiku, which captures single experiences, is not just in the present. The past continues to haunt or delight us and I've shared a few flashbacks I had to my childhood and youth in this volume, too.

I make no apology for touching on more "mundane" topics like health and well-being, since haiku is the language of the small worlds we inhabit, within the grander ones out there we cannot touch, or reach, accessible only through wonder, the poet's last refuge.

In conclusion, these days, it doesn't always seem politically correct to declare one's faith openly, so those who don't like to hear about another person's belief in God may not enjoy many haiku in *Rebirths* which refer to God, and that's okay, too.

Michael J. Lee

Cape Town

April 2021

1. A big beginning

In the void, Time ticked,
new-born, in hot wombs of space,
kissed by God's Spirit.

2. Rebirths

To be a new man
is a beautiful feeling,
born again from death.

3. A birth

Let the sun be born:
a clock of epochs ticking
eternally true.

4. Grounded

I stand firm in God,
for his eternal presence
holds all worlds in place.

5. Calm

The bushveld's deep peace
envelops us in silence:
beasts and stars at ease.

6. Law of love

Love's law times your heart:
plant love and reap happiness:
freely, peace-seeds fall.

7. First word

The voice of God spoke.
He said, "Love and live in peace."
His first word was love.

8. Named

Call all things by name.
Love gives a true name to all.
Say your name with love.

9. Satellite

Deep, dark sky sparkles,
a lone satellite orbits
an infinite sea.

10. Completeness

My body, mind, heart
grow in roots of well-being:
yielding completeness.

11. Oneness

Oneness is to God
as oceans, as outer space,
as heaven and earth.

12. Call of Africa

Over continents,
valleys and one thousand hills
came the call of home.

13. *Lifting up*

Lift his name higher,
lift his banner to the skies:
praise the Almighty.

14. *Equal love*

Let love be my core,
let the rule of law be true
equally for all.

15. *Daylight*

Balance at first light:
two birds sing to each other.
Let love shine through them.

16. *Treasures*

Art emboldened me:
music, paintings, pen and brush:
spiritual treasures.

17. *A true path*

If people won't love
I will love things: stones, rocks, thorns
and the paths to stars.

18. *A veld scene*

A warm and wet veld
awakes after light night rain:
I rise a new man.

---

19. *From above*

No love from above
ever dies, like earthly things
pass in suddenness.

20. *Adam*

Adam sneezed with dust
at ground zero; then sky breathed
God's air into him.

21. *On dust*

Dust can be stardust.
Walk humbly over earth's crust:
cosmos of powder.

22.   *A picture of the bush*

Bush-studded hills roll
to the horizon hosting
shy animal hordes.

23.   *The constant*

Strange how all things change
and fade, but what cannot age:
more timeless than stars.

24.   *Rejuvenation*

In slow, summer days
healing came to my worn heart,
when love made me whole.

25. *Believing*

Faith is being sure
of God's timeless existence
and plans for all life.

26. *Summer eve*

Under moon and stars,
in the pool, I feel so real:
held up by water.

27. *Reborn*

If I am reborn,
I'm a child of the cosmos:
made in His image.

28.   *In passing*

Paint the summer soon
in green and gold, blue and white:
before this time ends.

29.   *Conviction*

I banish all doubt
and fear of the unknown
to be reborn free.

30.   *Grace*

Give grace my best chance:
love beyond comprehension,
love so real, it heals.

31.   *Sometimes*

When fear hits home,
or sharp jabs of hate hurt me:
I pray for more light.

32.   *Forever*

Forever loving
is God: always cherishing
everything he's made.

33.   *An African rainfall*

Like living mercy,
African rain drizzles down,
defeating the heat.

34.   *First mist*

Mist grew from the sea
and rained on land washed by light,
giving birth to breath.

35.   *Tea*

A hot cup of tea
begins the new day for me,
giving strength to be.

36.   *Soil*

When fear abounds,
like a disease in the soil,
no strong fruit can grow.

37.   *Prayers*

Prayers are messages
our hearts send to heaven,
filled with secret hopes.

38.   *Scene in Addo game park*

On thorny, grass hills
thicket blankets orange soil
where herds roam their trails.

39.   *Sunny dream*

He who made the Sun,
made us, seeking light and life,
searchers for new earths.

40.   *A wish*

May hope be greater,
may love grow ever stronger,
may peace be deeper.

41.   *While troubles last*

Let your peace abide
while times of trouble prevail,
as sorrows test us.

42.   *To Abraham*

Abraham crossed lands
to answer the call of faith:
fathering nations.

---

43. *Breeze*

Come my friend the wind
blow cool air in my garden
after the heat wave.

44. *Daily news of the world*

Each dawn I hope more,
each day I see more sad news,
each eve I pray more.

45. *An evening scene in Durbanville*

A sickle moon rose.
Two guinea-fowl crossed the street:
wind-weary at dusk.

46. Sunshine

Sunshine on my head,
sending from far rays of hope:
balm for my bare feet.

47. Elements

Elements from God
make cosmic matter: moulded
into forms of life.

48. Hiding in holiness

I like to hide in
my spirit's secret shadows:
safe in holiness.

49.   *My childhood radio (i)*

Like a heart beating,
my radio pulsed signals
tuning me to worlds.

50.   *My childhood radio (ii)*

Songs and stories beamed,
hit parades on Friday nights:
broadcasting the Earth.

51.   *Cinema*

Cinema formed me,
freeing imagination...
to dream of new worlds.

———

52.   *Force of nature*

Love is a true force
no yearning heart can resist,
ruling like a law.

53.   *Freely*

I love so freely,
I pray so positively:
living hopefully.

54.   *A no-hate heart*

Look! my hate-free heart
helps me be a man of peace,
striving to spread love.

55. *Good preconditions*

There is zero chance
that creation was by chance:
everything in place!

56. *An interpretation of the Southern Cross*

I saw one weak light,
for us, embraced by three stars:
Father, Son, Spirit.

57. *Misty*

The morning mist dripped
across Ruitersbos valley:
fresh before first light.

58.   *Made well*

He who made all things,
made them well, with nature's laws
firmly established.

59.   *Three principles of wellness*

(i)   Health is beautiful.
(ii)   Sugar is anathema.
(iii) Exercise is youth.

60.   *The birth*

A baby is born.
A good man and woman smile,
dreaming of new times.

61.   Africa and I

In my dreams somewhere,
Africa came to my side,
bold as a lion.

62.   Elephant skulls

Two big, white skulls glint
on slopes of an old, green hill:
bones of grand beings.

63.   All bust up

Broken creatures search
in a broken world to heal,
hungry for love's balm.

64.   Tested

I bless each new day,
though it will surely test me
in life's crucible.

65.   Jesus

He touched history,
he changed human destiny:
his cross redeems pain.

66.   A private little tribute to Pierre Cardin

Dreams before money!
Married in a Cardin suit:
style for the masses!

67. Brief economics' lesson

If wealth makes more wealth,
if shared, it will multiply,
spreading happiness.

68. A thought about Time

If time moves forwards,
Past used to be the Future:
our destiny.

69. Heartbeat of peace

Give me truth and love
and I will understand life,
overcoming change.

70.   *New life*

Give me new life now,
not fading nostalgia.
Give me new blood now.

71. *Haiku of light*

At first, there was light:
to shape the formless gases
and rule all the days.

72.   *Jackal*

A black-backed jackal
leapt out of a taut thicket
and crossed the lone road.

73. *Asleep*

On a lazy day,
a gang of buffalo snoozed
low among bushes.

74. *Eco synthesis*

My heart keeps pumping,
my brain keeps ticking with life,
like rushing water.

75. *Kilimanjaro*

Kilimanjaro,
where I woke up, bathed my wounds:
there where game roamed free.

76.   Cleansed

New blood is needed,
healed on the cross of pure love
for fresh anointing.

77.   Psalm 1:1

Beady-eyed mockers
and steely-hearted scoffers:
step aside for hope.

78.   Stand firm

Wrestle against doubt,
combat negativity:
believe in life's worth.

79.   Undernourished heart

Set my heart free, God.
"For love to grow, let hate go.
Love validates you."

80.   How sweetly made

God gave dna
to identify all life:
each made in glory.

81.   On grasslands

Statuesque zebra
stand strong on old hills and plains
of dusty grasslands.

82. *Warthog cameo*

A creased, old warthog
kneels to nibble grass near us,
then waddles away.

83. *Falcon*

Proudly on its perch,
the peregrine falcon stares
into endless veld.

84. *Idea*

I think Africa
is a father: big and stern,
watching all its young.

85.   Sun power

I sat in the sun
for an afternoon hour,
charged up with power.

86.   Good start

I start each morning
in praise of the Creator,
with peace in my soul.

87.   Rule of law

A superorder
is beautiful to behold:
true only to truth.

88.   *Needs*

What do I need here?
Jesus was right – look to birds:
they know God cares well.

89.   *In the wild*

Addo made me new,
close to the bush's heartbeat,
pumping warm lifeblood.

90.   *Cognitive worship*

Loving and great God,
you fill my life with meaning,
directed to Truth.

91.   *In pain*

To all pain, answers
I do not have; but the cross
offers redemption.

92.   *A new pledge*

I'll run with your love
until the sun's light runs out:
to honour your name.

93.   *A thousand deaths*

Let the old year die,
and the old ways that don't work:
dying empires.

94. *Healer*

Let blood heal my wounds,
let faith cure all my fears,
let hopes mend all hearts.

95. *Never in vain*

It was not in vain
my redemption, new each day,
made for each morning.

96. *This fresh morning*

I had a deep sleep.
Good sleep equals good brain cleanse...
ready for action!

97.   *Unlimited*

In the days and years,
we're new in vitality,
circling the Sun.

98.   *Vital pulse*

Order seeks new life,
cells that grow, blood that can breathe,
to flow fresh in us.

99.   *Another good start*

In the Beginning
was the Word. And creation
spoke with one true voice.

100. *Sounds at a nature reserve*

Cease your striving, heart,
listen to a bird and plane
transcending limits.

101. *Beautiful order*

Wisdom and power
made the world bright in its time:
true and beautiful.

102. *Cushioned*

Cushioned in God's love,
creation is primed for growth
in time's new seasons.

103. *Who we are*

I am very me,
through DNA spread in cells:
you are very you.

104. *The kiss*

God kissed breath in us,
formed of clay, filled with being:
matter and spirit.

105. *Formed*

With blood and spirit
he made us, male and female,
formed in his image.

106. *The sunbather*

Bathing in late sun,
I toast lightly on both sides,
glowing in bright light.

107. *A story of South Africa*

Our land born in war,
our nation reborn in peace:
miracle rainbow.

108. *The sower*

Then God formed creatures,
in kinds, from earth particles,
sowing seeds, fruit, plants.

109. *Milkwood coastline*

Sturdy Cape milkwood
survives sand and salty air:
strong, like its people.

110. *Signs of times*

Time just moves forwards,
while history looks backwards.
Why not look ahead?

111. *At Keurbooms River, Garden Route*

Names and numbers speak
as one in the estuary,
blending sky and sea.

112.   Atom life

With atoms, God formed
all animals and humans:
dust and dna.

113.   Not bereft

Not bereft are we,
she left her harvest of love:
peace for new seasons.

114.   An example

Her example shines
from beyond the grave and sky:
"Love well, as I did."

115.   Mud

From mud we were made:
particles of creation
reused in aeons.

116.   After three o'clock

After three, the sun
pours out free Vitamin D
to bring well-being.

117.   New Year's eve

As a sad year ends,
let hope be undefeated:
faith in some future.

118. Eternal embrace

In the beginning
God wove time and space as one,
forever entwined.

119. Creating haiku

Like piano keys
I play single words in time
blended together.

120. View of Addo

A movie of clouds
rolled across the balcony:
ravens pecking crumbs.

121.   For the spekboom

Spekboom gives sweet leaves
in spiked thickets and creepers:
vital home biome.

122. Recycled

I was made in earth,
atoms and dust particles;
cosmic recycling.

123. Power of Rachmaninoff

Colourscapes of sound
filtering through my senses:
throbbing with power.

---

124. A grateful man

Safe in God I live:
no mean existence on earth
gloriously made.

125. Fairness

I count an angel
for every unfair person
who cheats another.

126. Stand up

Let's believe in us:
stand up, new South Africa,
for who we became.

127. *From whence love comes*

Burn the pain in flames
of pure love, old as light
from the dawn of time.

128. *What I know*

One thing I do know:
God gave so much grace to me:
more than I deserve.

129. *Trees*

Strong trees of knowledge,
loaded with smart dna,
know good from evil.

130. In praise

Fair beyond compare
is the immortal, true God:
who freely gives life.

131. The covid-19 Christmas

Insecurity
of food, shelter and future:
Christ born in a barn.

132. No greater belief

No greater belief
have I than my faith in God,
who's always with me.

---

133. *Time of the cross*

Come, all believers,
there's a time in history
that won us freedom.

134. *Airborne*

A brown hawk glided,
tail fanned above its talons,
speckled wings outspread.

135. *Against wrong*

Hold firm against wrong,
hold humans accountable,
myself included.

136. Known

God's speech was power,
giving names to all beings,
in lands wide and green.

137. A whole person

I wish to be whole.
Completeness is my life's goal:
stronger in intent.

138. Xenophobia

Are we all strangers?
Earth's dust birthed no foreigners:
empires made foes.

139. Heartbeat

I use time wisely,
like water, like food, like breath!
I time my heartbeats.

140. Made

He made worlds for love,
beauty signed in words of light:
handcrafted by love.

141. Millennia

Two thousand years passed:
your words and wounds bring healing
still to hurting hearts.

142. End of the beginning

Come alive again,
o weary world, rise up now:
art and life reborn.

143. Safe

Safe be my mother,
just as she looked after me:
safe be my mother!

144. Wife

Best friend of my soul
interwoven lives and minds:
dreams sealed as one.

145. *A mother's life well-lived*

Time is running out…
but no memory of mine
of your true goodness.

146. *A dark nostalgia*

Grumpy granddaddies
dream of bad past empires
and patriarchies…

147. *Art*

Art is free to be,
like me, escaping the past…
to be one with time.

148. *Living time*

One step at a time
because you're in the moment,
living your story.

149. *Australia's big history*

For millennia,
Aborigines lived free
on Australia.

150. *The smile*

Only let me smile
because my heart is beating
and new days bring hope.

151. Raptor

The hawk screams its call
out over the field of trees:
all small creatures hide.

152. Healing touch

God's love enfolds me,
stirring light in my spirit:
heal me with your touch.

153. Spiritual flowers

My Jesus, my life,
sow seeds of love in my soul
for flowers of peace.

154. Divisions

Across the divides,
Jesus builds bridges of peace,
paths of righteousness.

155. Meaning

I looked for meaning:
in the purposes of God
I found direction.

156. Positive and negative

Anxiety sucks,
but the love of God builds hope…
until my heart bursts.

157.   *Pandemic*

Bad news brings dark thoughts.
No! I am alive and free,
able to fight on.

158.   *Truth calls*

I'm a truth-seeker
becoming a truth-speaker...
his voice is gentle.

159.   *The searcher*

I seek all my days,
within circles and cycles,
our world in orbit.

———

160. *History renewed*

Order is living,
not owned by old empires:
history made new....

161. *A day is calling*

Work through each day well,
sow seeds of grace on the way:
everything's okay.

162. *Composure*

To anger, add peace,
for Cain became Earth's stranger,
a marked murderer.

163.   The dare

I dared call God mine,
when I first believed in him
who'd reached out his hand.

164.   At the start

Once upon a time
a power made all the worlds:
bless the name of God.

165.   A God called Majesty

My best hope is God.
What is my life next to God?
I choose majesty.

166. *Battle of the open field*

Territorial:
a hawk jostles with magpies
among blue gum trees.

167. *The mark of Cain*

Earth forgets not blood
that cries in the ground for peace,
where sad Cain wanders.

168. *Big Birth*

Time and space were born
in a super-explosion,
unleashing power.

169. *A heat wave ends*

Soft and cool rain falls,
lightly through heat's heavy air:
kisses for the grass!

170. *Overflow*

Peace is a fullness.
Joy is a deep contentment:
fearless am I.

171. *The guide*

Jesus is my guide
through life's trouble, pain and sin:
to the goal of grace.

172. *Self-improvement*

I must improve me:
increase caring and sharing
until love rules me.

173. *Southern creatures*

In the southern sun,
I seek my power to live:
creatures of pure light.

174. *Questions*

Am I relevant?
Will my work be meaningful?
I'll trust destiny.

175.   Rise of the ridiculous

Between the far left
and the ridiculous right
lies some Golden Mean.

176.   Goodness for all

Kindness, goodness, truth:
what else do I need for life,
to feed our lost souls?

177.   The renewed man

I'm new this new year.
I grew new roots and strong shoots
in body and mind.

178.   A new health

For my mint new mind,
I need a new, whole body,
fresh with renewed cells.

179.   More questions

Can I hold back tides?
Can I see infinity?
Can I touch my God?

180.   The fullness of peace

Creation is peace,
infused with God's peacefulness,
powered by all suns.

181.   *Wellness and discipline*

Let me cleanse myself
of metabolic stresses
from excess eating.

182.   *A deep renewal*

Wasted times and words?
Yes. Far too many to count....
Now, I am made new.

183.   *Voices*

Then God named all things.
And each name was personal:
each had a bright voice.

184. *Some positivity*

Whatever befalls,
it's free for humans to hope:
in the end, good wins.

185. *Beyond*

Beyond all concepts
and beyond all time, is God,
cradling existence.

186. *Where is the depth?*

This age deified
superficiality;
"Believe your own myths."

187.   A prayer

Irradiate sin,
cosmic God of earth and stars,
breathe your peace on us.

188.   Ideologues

Ideologues are...
bullies of the intellect,
puffed up by self-pride.

189.   On Munch's art

Munch and *angst* are as
ethereal Kafka's trial
tests senses and soul.

---

190. *Brokenness*

Broken parts re-used,
broken hearts with new purpose:
everything refreshed.

191. *Outdoors*

Feeling more alive
with sunshine over my skin
and wind through my hair.

192. *The first patent*

God owns the patent
to all creation he made:
all life is on loan.

193. *A game of names*

Mankind mastered speech
and gave names to animals,
naming everything.

194. *A sun's journey*

Let light time our days,
let suns clock all our years:
let progress be strong.

195. *A still scene in Plettenberg Bay*

Sunlight, so silent,
fills the sky with energy,
shore showered in peace.

196. Soli deo Gloria

Who made Earth so blue?
Soli deo Gloria!
Who made me and you?

197. Elements

Let creation rise
fresh from water and sunlight
to breathe free on Earth.

198. Cool sounds

Children's play echoes
over the hot, buzzing bush,
sun sizzling the pool.

199. River of time

Time is a river
freely flowing in the sea,
which makes rain again.

200. Reorientation

Whenever I'm lost,
re-orientate purpose:
love will lead us home.

201. Two gifts

Hearts beat and blood flows,
clocks tick, tides ebb and night comes:
time and breath are gifts.

202. Systems

From the brain to stars,
everything is a system.
How best can they work?

203. Little golf course scene

Four gentle rabbits
playing near the golf course greens:
coats shining like grass.

204. Inside

Inside is gentle,
made of soul fabric, softly:
what defence is there?

205. Moonshine

Rising into night,
its radiant reflection
rippled on the pool.

206. Healed man

Healed of pain, I'm whole,
remade again in power,
nourished by sunlight.

207. Misspent youth

I tried to grab life.
Now I feel my way forward,
with care, subtly.

208. Test of goodness

Battles for goodness
begin again each morning…
Let me choose sure ways.

209. Under strain

Let no courage fail,
let no hope shrink or cower,
let no true dream die.

210. Business philosophy

Methods and systems
are what makes the world work well:
run by team players.

211. *Looking up*

Without direction
you feel low, with no control:
look up for the way!

212. *Big deal*

To be forever
loved by God is a grand thing,
sheltering my heart.

213. *Heaven's world*

God is not the prince
of fickle human power:
for all time, He rules.

214. In times of strife

Giving up hope now,
in strife, isn't an option:
I'm healed of despair.

215. Silent solace

Sweet stars still sparkle
silently on moonless nights:
no storms hold me back.

216. Held

The world is broken,
but God's love never changes:
hold, while the wind howls.

217. Ban Sydney's new year fireworks

An incandescence
without substance or meaning...
do something useful.

218. Nationalism takes long to die

Nationalisms breed
on fringes of north borders
in old empires.

219. Transcendent

Royal is my God
who framed heavens in the sky,
loyal in his love.

———————

220. *Growing in confidence*

Assurance breeds peace.
Wellness boosts my confidence.
I live for wholeness.

221. *A summer renewal*

Wash me in new blood,
touch my skin with forgiveness,
heal me with sunlight.

222. *These three*

Hope lifted me high,
peace mellowed my restless mind,
love completing me.

223. Above all

Beyond what words say,
or what thoughts can understand,
is your glory, God.

224. Unlocked

Heal our old wounds,
birth new worlds of hope and love,
unchained from past wrongs.

225. Inner knowing

To see is to know,
to believe is to know why,
to hope is to trust.

226. Watching

I'd rather watch stars,
the movie of the cosmos,
than endless TV.

227. Blue day

It's okay I failed,
sleep's surreal dreams made me new
this lucid, blue day.

228. The surrender

Christ laid down his life,
giving us his right to live,
to free us from blame.

---

229. *This day*

When the morning comes,
I see goodness surrounds me:
provisions and gifts.

230. *And the winner is....*

Power beats fear,
order outperforms chaos,
goodness shines longest.

231. *A spectrum of earth*

I saw four prisms
for each corner of the world:
one light, all colours....

232. Giving

Forgiven, I rise,
strong with goodness for the day,
to give all I get.

233. Kudu cameo

The kudu's long horns,
too perfect to be branches,
peak above bushes.

234. Realisation

No more lost, wrong turns,
no more bad roads to nowhere:
bring God's love to all.

235. My guide

My heart's king is God:
may love's kindness guide my thoughts
to fill life with joy.

236. What's left

A child became stone,
all I've seen turned into dreams:
life is all that's left.

237. Overcoming

In God's bright power,
I rise above dark evil
to glow with sunshine.

238. Pledge

So great is your love,
Lord, I'll lay down ingrained hate
and old grievances.

239. Get real

Only sell what's real.
Brook no fancy theory,
believe no nonsense.

240. What was first?

In the beginning
was truth: God's laws of Nature,
time flowing forward.

___

241. With her

With her, we are two
on a journey to oneness,
as God intended.

242. Song of God

His truth is his word,
blessing creation with light,
loving what he made.

243. For Joe Biden

Let me be as brave
in ageing, as when younger:
yet stronger of mind.

244. Deconstruction

The unteachable
lived among us and became:
ungovernable.

245. True service

When the customer
isn't a commodity:
true, humane service.

246. As one

Systems in cycles,
for food and water supply,
tie nature to us.

247. The catharsis

He became a curse
and outcast pinned to a cross,
punished for this peace.

248. Sharing

Heal what is hurting!
Make whole all which is broken!
Give strength to the weak!

249. Borderlands

Born in borderlands...
where paranoid men still roam,
haunted by old wars.

250. *Peace and fear*

Peace is the one thing
no one can steal from your soul:
be strong, grow stronger.

251. *Grateful*

Goodness surrounds me,
God's grace freely upholds me:
sunlight makes me smile.

252. *Knowledge*

Keep knowledge living,
facts alive with life's essence:
embroidered patterns.

---

253. *Healing light*

Heal, Light, heal, shine long,
burn true, overcome all wrong:
show me the right way.

254. *Called to be*

Crazy, unfair world,
who would be born into it,
but one called by God?

255. *Who?*

Who carries their cross
willingly, that will kill them,
but the redeemer?

256. Cherished

Living, breathing Earth,
to all known life you gave birth:
I cherish your life.

257. To Rachmaninoff's Piano Concerto No. 2

Hypnosis touched pain
deep in his mind, unlocking
a rebirth of art.

258. Greatest

As light is fastest,
God's love is the greatest force:
ruling gravity.

259.   At my core

God is mine, I'm his,
a core bond none can open,
a truth none can steal.

260.   In the big garden

Take a time of peace
close to the living, green earth,
there by the mountain.

261.   On the move

Home is a vessel
on high seas of Time's changes:
lift higher your hopes.

---

262. Some tributes

Love made me believe,
music and film consoled me,
art taught me to dream.

263. Algorithms

Don't want to be trapped
by hidden algorithms
filtering my mind.

264. Without end

Inexhaustible
is my God's life, love and peace:
deeper than sunlight.

265. *Where love comes and goes*

Let love be honoured:
made in heaven to save earth,
binding all to all.

266. *A form of surrender*

Against loneliness
I lost the battle; relief
seeped deep in my soul.

267. *Faithful*

Faithful is my God,
who made us in his image,
healing all the lost.

268. Universal goodness

Goodness is the way:
creation is the real world
that holds true through all.

269. Hoping

God is on hope's side.
Hope is stronger than worry.
Hope glows in my heart.

270. The preserver

Lord of all living,
heal me, calm me, give me hope,
preserve me each day.

271. True life

My heart sings God's praise,
my breath calls out to True Life,
who is God most high.

272. Tribute to music

Rachmaninoff, Brahms
blew my mind with concertos;
while Handel just soared.

273. Evergreen

Our lives are like
Earth's endless water cycle,
ever renewing.

———————

274. *Mea culpa*

I should have cared more.
I should have made more effort.
I fell short, again.

275. *A blessing*

God blesses all life.
Let goodness reign over all:
may gentleness flow.

276. *Who?*

Who will push back tides?
Or stop flowers from blooming?
Who can stop God's love?

277. New day

Another day dawns.
A flock sails across the sky.
My mind is reborn.

278. Timeless

Beyond words is God,
at work in the universe:
formed in love and awe.

279. Improvement

Let's improve systems
to work better and fairer,
until the world blooms.

280. Cross

Christ's blood on the cross
will never be defeated:
it's shed for us all.

281. A self-portrait

If I face forward,
I can beat Time with purpose,
forged in bright fire.

282. One summer evening

The rest of the world
I don't need, here in Cape Town:
my home is complete.

283. Seven

The seventh moment
is pure rest, where peace will brood
and thankfulness reign.

284. Belonging

Beyond words God lives,
his love came to me one night,
calling me his own.

285. Living love

Set my spirit free,
let God love me to wellness:
I let go of me.

286. Recycling

All is evolving,
within a recycling world,
gentle as water.

287. Strangeness

How strange is this life:
fleeting, puzzling, beautiful;
say "So what?" and live!

288. The Word

And the Word was law.
And gravity ruled the worlds.
Then time flowed forwards.

———————

289. Humble

Ungodlike are we:
liken not human to God.
Seek his true glory.

290. Voids

When relations fail,
it can leave holes in your heart
only God can fill.

291. Sugary hell

One path to health hell
is paved with sugar candy.
Sign not your downfall.

292. Goodness

I support goodness.
Good is better than evil:
guard the rule of law...

293. Newton's praise

The Word was wisdom.
And it gave speech to science
and names to all life.

294. Transformation

All shame and shortfalls
you took and bore in your heart,
transforming all pain.

____

295. For my mother

God of stars and clouds,
bring my mother home to peace,
where her yearning led.

296. Go long, beloved mother

So long now, Mother,
you left behind enough love
for us to live on.

297. Our Father

The father of life
nurtures his sons and daughters
for eternity.

298. *If*

If I'm strong in God,
then why not believe *much more*
in him who loves me?

299. *Span of life*

From her womb inside
a room, I'm born to be free:
until this tomb shuts.

300. *If Time is God's*

God made Time begin
to put the days in order,
counted in heartbeats.

301. *A humble success*

Some daily progress
is all you need, to sleep well:
edging ever on.

302. *Timeless creation*

Who made me so real?
Life's an ancient mystery:
elements made whole.

303. *The old cross*

Across the ages
you reach out from your old cross,
torn wounds healing life.

304. Once upon a time on Earth

A home in the stars...
and all Nietzsche came up with
was nihilism.

305. Saved

A deep wish came true.
In my heart I hold a truth:
I'm a child of God.

306. The call

I heard a great call
to renew the creation:
who loves Earth the most?

307. Not yet there

Am I incomplete?
There's a path to completeness
I slowly follow.

308. What God gave

God, you gave me peace
the world didn't want to give:
a love that was lost.

309. Born homeless

Christ, born in a barn,
lives in his home in heaven
and in loving hearts.

310. The exemplar

He taught us to serve.
He showed how far love can go.
His name is Jesus.

311. War and peace

The weapon of peace
is a cross which hanged a man,
injured for all wounds.

312. Saviour

I celebrate Christ
whose influence is immense:
spanning history.

313. *Made new again*

All the pain's paid for,
all loads, all my wrong and blame:
in peace of Jesus.

314. *Yielding*

I yield to you, God:
superior and supreme
in strength, love, goodness.

315. *A dawn*

Let God carry worlds,
upholding us in spirit,
as we rise to life.

316. *What matters*

Goodness matters most.
Even wisdom serves goodness:
heaven's grace on Earth.

317. *No giving up*

No wall holds out love,
no problem can defeat hope:
forever love dreams.

318. *Yet more hope*

Hope abounds with God,
whose light rules each day and night,
who underpins things.

———

319. *Forever and ever*

Grace is to God as
air belongs to atmospheres,
flooding through Nature.

320. *Creation's code*

Founded on wisdom,
Nature spoke the truth of laws,
coded for splendour.

321. *Love's dream*

Love is the real dream,
colouring the world in light:
life reimagined.

322. *A refreshing*

Let my soul be new,
let my deep hopes be reborn,
let new work begin.

THE END

TITLES BY THE AUTHOR

SCIENCE FICTION

Chrysalis: A surgical sci-fi story about immortal potential

Lord of the Bats

Earthrise 2036

DOCUMENTARY NOVEL

Heartbeat

POEMS

Three Hundred and Twenty-One Haiku

Not Yet in Heaven

Rebirths

PLAYS

The Archive - a play about the last days of Friedrich Nietzsche

NON-FICTION

Passage to Faith

A New Logic For Faith

The Courage to Believe

FUTURE STUDIES

Codebreaking our Future

Knowing our Future

www.beyondheads.com
www.michaeljlee.com
michael@positivedestiny.org

About the Author

Michael J. Lee, Master of Philosophy (Futures Studies) (cum laude), Master of Arts in English, Honours-Baccalaureus Theologiae (cum laude), Higher Education Diploma (with distinction).

Michael enjoys reading, writing, painting, sketching, jogging and watching powerful movies, having built up a private collection of several hundred DVDs and Blu-ray films spanning the entire history of cinema to the present. He has been married to Sannettha since 1990 and the couple have two daughters, Michaela, a food and cosmetic scientist, and Melissa, a linguist and business analyst.

Lee has been CEO of the ATM Industry Association (www.atmia. com), which has over 11,000 members in about 70 countries, since 2005. He is chairperson of the Consortium for Next Gen ATMs which has over 400 companies participating in this future-proofing exercise to link over 3 million ATMs with more than 5 billion mobile phones.

Michael is a qualified futurist, artist and writer living in Cape Town. In 2015, he published *Heartbeat,* a documentary novel about the world's first human heart transplant. His two works about understanding the social future through interdisciplinary causal analysis are *Knowing our Future* and *Codebreaking our Future,* both available on Amazon.com.

He has written three science fiction works, *Chrysalis,* a story about the world's first head transplant, and *Earthrise 2036,* a part-documentary, part-imaginary journey through the evolution of humanity from the rawest of origins in the Cradle of Humankind to the age of space exploration, and *Lord of the Bats,* the sequel to *Chrysalis.*